QUANTITATIVE TRADING SECRET

SECRET

The secret strategies of profitable trading

Ben Henry

Copyright © 2023 by Ben Henry

Disclaimer

This book is designed to provide condensed information. It's not intended to reprint all the information that is otherwise available, but instead to complement, amplify and supplement other texts. You are urged to read all available materials, learn as much as possible and tailor the information to your individual needs.

The purpose of this book is to educate.

Table of Contents

FOREWORD

Trading is one of the world's oldest and most challenging professions, and for good reason. The markets are complex, constantly shifting, and often difficult to navigate. Successful traders must have a deep understanding of economics, finance, and human behavior, as well as a keen ability to analyze data and make quick decisions under pressure.

Quantitative trading, the use of mathematical models and algorithms to make investment decisions, is one of the most powerful tools in a trader's arsenal. By incorporating quantitative analysis into their decision-making process, traders can identify potentially profitable opportunities that might otherwise go unnoticed, and execute trades with precision and efficiency.

The field of quantitative trading has grown rapidly in recent years, with many financial institutions and individual investors turning to these sophisticated systems to help them make informed investment decisions. These systems are designed to provide a competitive advantage in the world of finance, and can help investors to identify profitable trading opportunities more quickly and accurately than traditional manual processes.

That being said, the world of quantitative trading is often shrouded in secrecy, with many traders keeping their secrets and techniques closely guarded. This is why "Quantitative Trading Secret" is such a valuable resource. It provides an in-depth look at the world of quantitative trading, exploring the history, strategies, and ethics of this complex and often misunderstood field.

Whether you're a seasoned trader or just starting out, "Quantitative Trading Secret" offers insights and strategies that can help you take your trading game to the next level. By mastering the secrets of quantitative trading, you can gain an edge in a crowded and competitive market, and position yourself for long-term success. It is not only a valuable resource for traders, but also for anyone looking to gain insight into the financial industry and the role of quantitative trading in modern investing.

In this book, we will explore the secrets of successful quantitative trading, covering topics such as risk management, fundamental and technical analysis, and advanced topics in quantitative trading. We will delve into the intricacies of each topic, providing insights into how to develop successful strategies and incorporate them into your investment portfolio.

Whether you're a professional or just interested in the world of trading, I encourage you to take a journey through "Quantitative Trading Secret" and experience the power of quantitative trading for yourself.

So if you are serious about improving your trading decisions and maximizing your returns, then this book is for you. Let us explore the world of quantitative trading together and reveal the secrets of success in this dynamic and exciting field.

ACKNOWLEDGMENT

I would like to express my gratitude to all those who have helped me along the way in the development of this book.

First and foremost, I would like to thank the traders who are willing to share their secrets and strategies. Without your generosity and willingness to share your knowledge, this book would not be possible that you made this book.

Second, I want to thank my friends and family for their support and encouragement throughout this process. Your belief in me and your constant encouragement kept me motivated and focused.

Finally, I thank you, the reader, for giving me the opportunity to share my knowledge and experience with you. I hope that what you read here will inspire you to pursue your own dreams, and that the secrets and strategies shared in this book will help you achieve success in quantitative trading.

Once again, thank you all for your support, and I hope that you find this book to be both informative and engaging.

1

A BRIEF HISTORY OF QUANTITATIVE TRADING

There has been a long and illustrious history of quantitative trading, where investment decisions are made using computer models and algorithms. The development of quantitative trading dates back to the late 1940s and into the early 1950s, when John Von Neumann, Stanislas Ulam, and other mathematicians and physicists began developing mathematical models that could be used for trade. These models, at the start of their existence, were mainly aimed at analyzing historical price data in order to identify patterns and trends.

More advanced technical models and algorithms, including the development of Black Scholes option pricing theory and Random Walk Theory that suggest stock prices are driven by an unpredictable pattern over time, were developed in the 1960s and 1970s. The rise of high frequency trading, whereby traders use powerful computers to perform trades at extremely fast speeds according to sophisticated algorithms and models, occurred over the 1980s and 1990s as a result of development of computer and algorithmic trading.

Alex had always been fascinated by the world of financial markets, spending countless hours researching different market trends and analyzing data. As he explored the world of trading, he became increasingly interested in the potential of quantitative trading, which promised to help traders make informed investment decisions based on mathematical models and algorithms.

Determined to learn more about quantitative trading, Alex devoured every book, article, and online course he could find on the subject. He spent countless hours poring over market data, experimenting with different algorithms, and refining his strategies.

The more Alex learned, the more he realized that he had a knack for quantitative trading. He was able to spot patterns and trends that eluded other traders, and he developed a keen ability to identify profitable opportunities. With his newfound skills, Alex established himself as a respected trader, regularly outperforming the market and leaving his competitors in the dust.

As he continued to expand his skills and grow his trading account, Alex remained focused on his goal of using quantitative trading to generate long-term wealth. He continued to study and experiment, constantly refining his strategies and always looking for ways to improve. And with his unwavering commitment to learning and growing, Alex was able to secure a place for himself at the forefront of the quantitative trading world, serving as an inspiration to other traders and demonstrating the enormous potential of this powerful approach to investment.

2

THE IMPORTANCE OF TRADING SECRETS

In the world of business and investment, trading secrets are important because they enable traders to have an advantage in terms of competition as well as allowing them to make informed investment decisions. Without these secrets, traders might not be able to obtain the information necessary for their respective decisions and could lose a considerable amount of money. Furthermore, the value of trading secrets for traders in order to distinguish themselves from their competitors and attract potential clients may be significant.

It is therefore important for traders to maintain the confidentiality of their secrets, especially in a highly competitive environment, so that they may not share them with others. But it's worth noting that secrets can be difficult to conceal, which may give rise to a danger of being lost if traders don't care about their information. Finally, it cannot be underestimated what a crucial role trade secrets play within the investment and commercial world; traders have to take all necessary steps to keep their secrets safe.

In order to maintain competitive advantage, it is also necessary to have trading secrets in addition to providing traders with an edge on the market. The traders will distinguish themselves from their competitors by keeping secrets and knowledge private, thus attracting clients. This will increase their revenue, but it is also helping them distinguish themselves as experts in the area of trade.

In addition, traders may be helped by the knowledge of trade secrets to find and exploit undiscovered opportunities on the market. It is possible for traders to make an important profit in a market through analyses of vast amounts of data and the analysis of patterns and trends that others might miss. This is particularly relevant for volatile markets, as the ability to respond quickly to change market conditions can have a decisive effect on success or failure.

But, of course, there are risks involved in the trade secrets. Traders need to take care of the security of their secrets since any breach could lead to loss of an advantage and a decrease in competition. In addition, entrepreneurs may miss opportunities for collaboration and synergy that can enable them to achieve more success in the market if they keep their secrets. Therefore, the balance of keeping a secret and exchanging information must be struck by traders to strike a balance between keeping their secrets and sharing information to maximize their potential in the market.

STATISTICAL AND MACHINE LEARNING

Quantitative trading is a type of financial trading that involves using statistical and machine learning models to analyze data and make investment decisions. The goal of quantitative trading is to identify patterns and trends in the market that can be used to generate profitable trades without relying solely on human intuition.

Statistical models are one of the key components of quantitative trading. These models utilize statistical analysis to identify patterns in market data, such as stock prices, interest rates, and exchange rates. The models can be used to develop strategies for trading, such as mean reversion, trend following, or dividend yield strategies.

Machine learning is another important component of quantitative trading. Machine learning models can be trained on large datasets of historical market data to identify patterns and trends that can inform investment decisions. For example, a machine learning model can be trained to identify stock price patterns that indicate an upcoming rebound in the market.

The combination of statistical and machine learning models can be powerful in quantitative trading, as they can provide traders with access to a wealth of data and insights that might be difficult to identify by other means. However, it's important to note that quantitative trading can be a complex and highly technical field, and it's important for traders to have a solid understanding of both statistical and machine learning concepts to be successful.

The use of statistical and machine learning in quantitative trading has revolutionized the way in which financial markets operate. These technologies are able to analyze vast amounts of data, identify patterns, and make predictions with incredible accuracy. This has had a significant impact on the trading industry, with many funds and institutions now using quantitative trading strategies to allocate resources and make investment decisions.

Statistical and machine learning are particularly useful in high-frequency trading, where decisions must be made in a matter of microseconds. In this type of trading, the ability to analyze market data and make predictions is critical, and statistical and machine learning techniques are particularly well suited to this task. Through the use of algorithms and mathematical models, traders are able to identify market patterns and trends much faster than a human could, giving them a significant advantage over other investors.

DATA ANALYSIS

Data analysis is a critical component of quantitative trading, as it is used to identify patterns and trends in the market that can be used to make trading decisions. In quantitative trading, data is collected from a variety of sources, including historical market data, news articles, and social media conversations, and is analyzed using statistical and machine learning techniques.

One of the main goals of data analysis in quantitative trading is to identify relationships between different market variables that can be used to make predictions about future market trends. For instance, by analyzing historical stock prices, traders can identify patterns that may indicate a stock is undervalued or overvalued. By using statistical models such as regression analysis or machine learning algorithms like neural networks, traders can then make predictions about the direction of the stock price in the future.

Another important aspect of data analysis in quantitative trading is data cleaning and preprocessing. Raw data may contain errors or inconsistencies that can bias the results of any analysis. To address these issues, traders must clean and preprocess the data to ensure that it is accurate and reliable. This may involve removing missing values, transforming data to a usable format, or imputing missing values based on statistical methods.

An important aspect of data analysis in quantitative trading is also backtesting. Backtesting involves testing a trading strategy on historical data to evaluate its performance and identify any potential issues that may arise in the future. This allows traders to fine-tune their strategies and ensure they are performing as expected before implementing them in live markets.

Overall, data analysis plays a critical role in quantitative trading, and the ability to analyze large amounts of data quickly and accurately can provide traders with a significant competitive edge in today's financial markets. With the ongoing evolution of statistical and machine learning techniques, data analysis in quantitative trading is only going to become more powerful and sophisticated in the years to come.

The use of visualization tools is also important for data analysis in quantitative trading. Visualization can help traders to quickly understand the patterns and relationships present in the data, and it's an essential tool for exploring large datasets and identifying trends.

Data analysis is a crucial component of quantitative trading, and the ability to analyze large amounts of data quickly and accurately is essential for traders to succeed in today's financial markets..

5

AIGORITHMIC TRADING TECHNIQUES

Algorithmic trading is a type of quantitative trading that involves using automated software programs to execute trades based on predefined criteria and strategies. In algorithmic trading, algorithms are used to analyze market data and make investment decisions in real-time, allowing traders to take advantage of pricing inefficiencies and market fluctuations.

Algorithmic trading techniques can range from simple rule-based strategies to advanced machine learning models, and traders can choose from a variety of different types of algorithms based on their specific trading goals and objectives. Some common algorithmic trading techniques include volume-based strategies, moving average crossover strategies, trend-following strategies, and arbitrage strategies. Volume-based strategies involve analyzing the volume of trading activity and using it as a signal to enter or exit a trade. Moving average crossover strategies involve comparing the price of a security to a moving average and making a trade when the price crosses above or below the average. Trend-following strategies involve following market trends and making trades in the direction of the trend. Arbitrage strategies involve identifying pricing inefficiencies between markets and taking advantage of them for profit.

By using algorithmic trading techniques, traders can automate their trading processes and make quick, data-driven decisions in a constantly evolving market environment. This can help traders reduce their emotional involvement in trading decisions and make more rational and calculated decisions based on data analysis. However, traders should always be aware of the potential risks involved in algorithmic trading, such as the risk of software errors or market fluctuations that can adversely affect trading results.

In addition to algorithmic trading, another essential component of quantitative trading is high-frequency trading (HFT). HFT involves using advanced algorithms to execute trades at extremely high speeds, sometimes with durations of just a few milliseconds. HFT is commonly used by hedge funds and investment firms to take advantage of market microstructure inefficiencies and make profits from small price movements.

HFT algorithms are designed to analyze market data quickly and identify opportunities for profit in real-time. These algorithms are often based on complex mathematical models and use advanced data analysis techniques to make predictions about future market trends. HFT algorithms are also designed to minimize latency and execute trades as quickly as possible, giving them a competitive advantage over slower trading strategies.

SECRET TRADING TECHNIQUES

Secret trading techniques are proprietary strategies or methods used by traders to gain an edge in the market and generate consistent returns. These techniques are often closely guarded by traders and may be kept as a closely-held family secret, shared only with trusted friends or business associates.

Some common secret trading techniques include technical analysis, fundamental analysis, and position trading. Technical analysis involves analyzing past price data to identify patterns and trends that can be used to predict future market movements, while fundamental analysis involves analyzing a company's financial statements and other quantitative data to make investment decisions. Position trading involves holding a trade for a longer period of time, usually several days or weeks, and waiting for the market to move in the desired direction before closing the position.

Another common secret trading technique is scalping, which involves making small profits on short-term investments through high-frequency trading. Scalping can be profitable, but it requires a high level of skill and a deep understanding of market trends and market microstructure.

Another common secret trading technique is arbitrage, which involves taking advantage of small pricing discrepancies between different markets or assets. Arbitrage can be profitable, but it requires a high level of market knowledge and the ability to quickly detect and capitalize on fleeting opportunities.

Secret trading techniques can be powerful tools for traders, but they can also be risky and complex. Traders must carefully consider the potential risks involved and ensure that their techniques are disciplined and well-managed. They must also have a backup strategy in case their secret trading technique is compromised or no longer profitable.

Overall, secret trading techniques can be a valuable resource for traders seeking a competitive edge in the market, but they must be used with caution and discipline. It's essential for traders to fully understand the potential risks involved and to develop a robust and well-rounded trading strategy that takes into account market conditions, portfolio risk, and personal investment goals.

7

THE PSYCHOLOGY OF SECRET TRADING

The psychology of secret trading involves the study of the emotional and psychological factors that influence traders' decisions to keep their trading strategies proprietary. Some common psychological factors that may contribute to secret trading include:

1. Fear of failure: Traders may fear that their secret trading strategy will fail or become obsolete, rendering their hard-earned knowledge and expertise worthless.

2. Fear of theft: Traders may fear that their strategies will be stolen or copied by competitors, resulting in a loss of competitive advantage.

3. Fear of criticism: Traders may fear that their strategies will be criticized by others or found to be ineffective, undermining their confidence and creating self-doubt.

4. Need for control: Traders may feel a need to control their trading strategy and decisions, believing that sharing their knowledge with others may result in a loss of control or a loss of independence.

5. Lack of trust: Traders may not trust that others will keep their secret trading strategies safe or may fear that they will

be taken advantage of by others seeking to profit from their hard work and ingenuity.

To overcome the psychological factors that may contribute to secret trading, traders can adopt a variety of strategies, including:

1. Creating a supportive and trusting network of traders who can provide constructive feedback and support.

2. Taking steps to protect their trade secrets and strategies, such as using non-disclosure agreements or other forms of legal protection.

3. Practicing open-mindedness and humility, recognizing that their knowledge and expertise are not the only ones that hold value.

4. Reminding themselves of the potential benefits of sharing their knowledge and expertise, such as building relationships and enhancing their personal and professional development.

5. Developing a growth mindset, believing that their knowledge and expertise are always evolving and that they have the power to continue learning and growing as traders.

Overall, the psychology of secret trading can be a complex and nuanced topic, and traders must carefully consider the implications of their actions and the impact they may have on their emotional state and trading performance. It's essential for traders to strike a balance between protecting their trade secrets and strategies while remaining open to sharing knowledge and expertise with others, ultimately finding the right balance for their individual goals and needs.

SECRET TRADING MINDSET

The secret trading mindset is the set of values, beliefs, and attitudes that traders hold about the importance of keeping their trading strategies secret and proprietary. These beliefs can have a significant impact on their trading performance and their ability to generate consistent returns over time.

Some common beliefs held by traders who embrace a secret trading mindset include:

1. Individuality and independence: Traders who embrace a secret trading mindset tend to value individuality and independence, believing that their success depends on their ability to stay one step ahead of the competition.

2. Knowledge and expertise: traders who embrace a secret trading mindset believe that their knowledge and expertise are rare and valuable, and that keeping their trading strategies proprietary is crucial to maintaining an edge in the market.

3. Control and ownership: Traders who embrace a secret trading mindset tend to feel a need for control and ownership over their trading strategies and decisions, believing that sharing their knowledge and expertise may result in a loss of control or a loss of personal identity.

4. Resourcefulness and perseverance: Traders who embrace a secret trading mindset tend to be highly resourceful and determined, believing that their ability to protect and maintain their trading strategies is a reflection of their skill and ability as traders.

To cultivate a secret trading mindset, traders may engage in a variety of practices, including:

1. Continuously learning and gathering knowledge: Traders who embrace a secret trading mindset value knowledge and expertise, actively seeking out ways to improve their understanding of the market and their trading strategies.

2. Staying competitive and innovative: Traders who embrace a secret trading mindset understand the importance of staying ahead of the competition, constantly adapting and improving their trading strategies to maintain an edge.

3. Building and maintaining a trading culture: Traders who embrace a secret trading mindset work to create a supportive and trusting network of traders who can provide feedback and support, as well as to share their knowledge and expertise in a responsible and deliberate manner.

4. Focusing on self-reflection and growth: Traders who embrace a secret trading mindset strive to develop a growth mindset, believing that their knowledge and expertise are constantly evolving and that they have the power to continue learning and growing as traders.

SECRET TRADING RESULTS

The secret trading results are the performance metrics that traders who keep their strategies proprietary strive to achieve in their trading activities. These results are often closely guarded and can include a range of performance indicators, such as:

1. Returns on investment (ROI): Secret trading results often include the actual returns that traders generate from their proprietary trading strategies. This can include metrics such as percentage gains, absolute gains, and annual returns.

2. Risk-adjusted returns: Secret trading results often emphasize risk-adjusted returns, reflecting the relationship between returns and risk. This can include metrics such as the Sharpe ratio, Sortino ratio, and information ratio.

3. Trading frequency: Secret trading results may include metrics that reflect the frequency of trades, including the number of trades made per day, week, or month.

4. Trade accuracy: Secret trading results may include metrics that reflect the accuracy of traders' trades, including the percentage of winning trades and the percentage of profitable trades.

5. Trade duration: Secret trading results may include metrics that reflect the duration of traders' trades, including the average holding period for each trade.

6. Trading discipline: Secret trading results may include metrics that reflect the discipline of traders' trade execution, including metrics such as the percentage of trades that follow trading rules, the maximum drawdown experienced, and the number of trades that are exited early.

7. Mental endurance: Secret trading results may include metrics that reflect a trader's mental resilience and ability to withstand the emotional challenges of trading, including metrics such as the frequency of emotional trading, the impact of stress on trading performance, and the degree of self-control and discipline demonstrated in trading.

To achieve secret trading results, traders need to develop trading strategies that are highly optimized for specific market conditions, have defined entry and exit criteria, and are executed with discipline and consistency. This requires a high level of skill, expertise, and emotional control, as well as a willingness to constantly adapt and improve their trading strategies over time.

LEGAL AND REGULATORY CONSIDERATION

Legal and regulatory considerations are an essential aspect of quantitative trading, particularly when it comes to the development, implementation, and operation of trading algorithms and strategies. Traders need to understand the regulatory environment they operate in to ensure they comply with applicable securities laws and regulations and minimize financial and legal risks.

Here are some common legal and regulatory considerations for quantitative traders to keep in mind:

1. Securities laws and regulations: Traders must comply with securities laws and regulations governing trading activities, including regulation in the country in which they operate. This may include requirements to register as a broker-dealer, investment advisor, or other type of financial services firm, as well as compliance with any reporting, disclosure, and record-keeping requirements.

2. Trading algorithms and strategies: Traders must ensure that their trading algorithms and strategies comply with

securities laws and regulations, including requirements for market manipulation, front-running, and other forms of illegal trading activity. For example, high-frequency traders must comply with regulations around "spoofing," which involves placing orders with the intent to cancel them before execution.

3. Data confidentiality and privacy: Traders must comply with data confidentiality and privacy laws and regulations, including requirements to protect sensitive data, such as customer information and proprietary trading strategies, from unauthorized access, disclosure, and use.

4. Cybersecurity: Traders must ensure that their trading systems are secure from cyber threats, including hacking, data breaches, and other forms of cyber attacks. This requires a robust cybersecurity infrastructure, including firewalls, encryption, and regular security monitoring and testing.

5. Financial reporting: Traders must comply with financial reporting requirements, including requirements to file quarterly and annual financial statements, as well as disclosure of material events and information to shareholders and investors.

6. Anti-corruption: Traders must comply with anti-corruption laws and regulations, including requirements to prevent bribery and kickbacks, money laundering, and other forms of corrupt business practices.

7. International trading: Traders operating in multiple jurisdictions must be aware of and comply with the unique

legal and regulatory requirements in each country, which can vary widely.

To navigate these legal and regulatory considerations, quantitative traders may need to seek the advice of legal and compliance professionals, including experienced attorneys, compliance consultants, and regulatory experts. In addition, trading firms may need to invest in technology solutions that provide risk management tools and compliance monitoring capabilities to mitigate legal and regulatory risks and ensure compliance.

In addition to complying with legal and regulatory requirements, trading firms must also consider the ethical implications of their trading activities and ensure that their strategies are aligned with industry standards and best practices. Here are some ethical considerations for quantitative traders to keep in mind:

1. Fairness and non-discrimination: Traders must ensure that their trading strategies are fair and non-discriminatory, and that they do not discriminate against any individuals or groups. This may include requirements to comply with anti-discrimination laws, such as Title VII of the Civil Rights Act in the United States, which prohibits discrimination on the basis of race, color, religion, sex, or national originality.

2. Conflict of interest: Traders must avoid engaging in activities that may create conflicts of interest, such as trading on insider information, manipulating financial markets for

personal gain, or engaging in self-trading or other forms of prohibited trading.

3. Environmental, social, and governance (ESG) considerations: Traders may consider incorporating ESG factors into their trading strategies, including environmental impact, social implications, and governance practices of the companies they trade. ESG factors can impact the performance and reputation of the firms they trade and the industries they operate in.

4. Transparency: Traders should strive to operate in a transparent and accountable manner, providing clear and accurate information to customers and regulators. This may include disclosing information about the firms they work for, the trading strategies they implement, and any potential conflicts of interest.

5. Diversity, equity, and inclusion: Traders should prioritize diversity, equity, and inclusion in their workforce, products, and services. This can include creating a workplace that values and promotes diversity and inclusivity, supporting equal pay and opportunity, and developing products and services that meet the needs of diverse customers.

Quantitative traders and the trading firms they work for must navigate a complex legal and regulatory landscape, as well as consider the ethical implications of their trading activities. To achieve both financial and ethical success, traders need to build robust risk management systems, comply with applicable laws and regulations, and prioritize transparency and accountability.

Conclusion

Quantitative trading, sometimes called algorithmic trading or program trading, is a systematic and automated approach to trading financial instruments, such as stocks, futures, options, and commodities. Quantitative traders use algorithms, models, and statistical analysis to develop trading strategies and identify patterns in market data to inform trading decisions. These algorithms are typically programmed to execute trades in real-time, allowing traders to react to changing market conditions and capture inefficiencies quickly and accurately.

Here are some of the key things to know about quantitative trading:

1. Types of algorithms: Quantitative traders use a variety of algorithms to identify trading opportunities and make decisions. These algorithms may be designed to analyze factors such as market trends, historical patterns, volatility, and risk-reward ratios. Some common types of algorithms include reinforcement learning, neural networks, and genetic algorithms.

2. Machine learning and artificial intelligence: Quantitative trading relies heavily on machine learning and artificial intelligence techniques to analyze large amounts of data and make predictions about future market movements. Machine learning algorithms are used to build models that capture

patterns and relationships in market data, while artificial intelligence is used to develop algorithms that can learn from repeated trading scenarios and adjust their decision-making frameworks over time.

3. Data sources: Quantitative trading requires access to a wide range of data sources, including market data, economic indicators, and news feeds. Traders may use real-time data streams to make decisions in near real-time, or historical data to develop models and test strategies. Some common data sources include financial statements, historical prices, and market indicators such as the CPI, GDP, and interest rates.

4. Risk management: Quantitative trading involves significant risk, and traders must have effective risk management systems in place to minimize potential losses. These systems may include risk tolerances, stop-loss orders, and position sizing strategies. Traders may also monitor their trades in real-time and adjust their strategies accordingly to avoid losses.

5. Regulatory requirements: As with any trading activity, quantitative traders must comply with applicable securities laws and regulations in the countries in which they operate. This may include requirements to register with regulators, comply with reporting and disclosure requirements, and maintain appropriate record-keeping systems.

Quantitative trading is a complex and powerful approach to trading that requires a deep understanding of market data, algorithms, risk management, and regulatory requirements. While the potential returns for successful quantitative traders are significant, the risks involved are also substantial. Therefore, traders must educate themselves

Quantitative trading has emerged as a powerful tool in the financial industry, allowing traders to use algorithms and data analysis to identify trading opportunities and execute trades with precision and efficiency. By leveraging sophisticated models, machine learning techniques, and artificial intelligence, traders can analyze market trends and patterns in real-time, making decisions that can potentially lead to high returns.

Quantitative trading requires a deep understanding of market data and algorithms, as well as thorough risk management strategies to mitigate potential losses. Traders must also be aware of the legal and regulatory requirements of their jurisdictions, including securities laws and regulations, market manipulation laws, and anti-corruption laws.

In conclusion, quantitative trading offers significant potential for traders who are skilled, strategic, and disciplined. While there are risks associated with any trading activity, quantitative trading can be a powerful tool for traders who are prepared to invest the time and resources necessary to master it. As with any trading activity, traders must always perform due diligence, seek assistance from experienced professionals as needed, and be prepared to adjust their strategies as market conditions and regulatory requirements evolve.